POTTERY TREASURES

Waters jars (canteens) of this type were used extensively throughout the Southwest during prehistoric times. Effigy handles were often a feature of Tularosa Black-on-white pottery made in the mountain and high plateau areas of East-central Arizona and West-central New Mexico between A.D. 1100 and 1250.

POTTERY TREASURES

The Splendor of Southwest Indian Art

Photography by Jerry Jacka
Text by Spencer Gill

International Standard Book Number 0-912856-28-9
Library of Congress Catalog Number 76-657
Copyright © 1976 by Graphic Arts Center Publishing Co.
2000 N.W. Wilson • Portland, Oregon 97209 • 503/224-7777

The ancient people of the Mimbres region of Southwestern
New Mexico are noted for their fine pottery, decorated with
unusual animal and human forms as well as carefully
executed geometric designs. These four Mimbres Black-on-
white bowls date between A.D. 1050 and 1200.

The jar and bowl are Gila Polychrome. Bird effigy, at the right, is Tonto Polychrome. This pottery was made between A.D. 1300 and 1450 by the Salado Indians, ancient dwellers of the deserts and mountain foothills of central Arizona.

Pottery of the ancient Hohokam, dwellers of the deserts of central Arizona. Jars are Sacaton Red-on-buff (A.D. 900-1100) and the flared rim bowl at the right is Santa Cruz Red-on-buff (A.D. 700-900).

Three examples of Sikyatki Polychrome made between A.D. 1375 and 1625 by the ancestors of the present-day Hopi Indians. This style of pottery was revived by Hopi potters toward the end of the 19th century and continues to be produced today.

Mesa Verde Black-on-white pottery made between A.D. 1200 and 1300. Excellent Examples of prehistoric mugs found in the Mesa Verde region are at the top.

Maria Martinez, the famous potter of San Ildefonso Pueblo examines one of her pottery treasures.

Acoma Pueblo, the "Sky City," sits high atop a stone mesa and is one of the oldest continually inhabited settlements in the United States.

Cochiti pottery of the late 1800's. The rawhide band tied around the rim of the large jar (in back) was a method of preventing further breakage of cracked vessels.

An unusually large and fine example of San Ildefonso pottery of the late 1800's.

Kachinas are often used as design elements for Hopi pottery. This old large Palhik Mana (Butterfly Kachina Maiden) kachina doll stands next to a Polacca Polychrome jar which was made at First Mesa on the Hopi reservation during the 1880's.

Polacca Polychrome pottery made in the Hopi area during the second half of the 19th century. The old rattle which contains a frog design and the hand woven belt were used during Hopi ceremonials.

Hopi pottery of the early 1900's. Jar at right is by Nampeyo, who is credited with the rebirth of Sikyatki Polychrome styling and the revival of fine craftsmanship in Hopi pottery making. Pieces of pottery tile are decorated with Hopi kachina designs and were collected by the Fred Harvey Company during 1913.

A fine example of old Acoma "four color" polychrome pottery made around 1890, contains a classic example of the Acoma stylized parrot. This jar, or "bread olla" as these large jars were sometimes called, is 17" high and 18¾" in diameter.

Tesuque "Rain Gods". These figurines had no ceremonial significance and represent the earliest example of pottery curios. The large micaceous figure at the left was made around 1900. The two at the right were made later, during the early 1900's.

Jars made between 1880 and 1900 display outstanding examples of geometric design elements which appeared on Acoma pottery during the late nineteenth century.

Hopi polychrome pottery by the Nampeyo family. Large jar at top left was made, circa 1900, by Nampeyo; her daughter, Fannie made the small wedding vase during 1975; her granddaughter, Leah, made the jar in the center in 1971. Jar at far right was molded by Nampeyo and painted by her daughter, Annie, during the early 1900's.

20

Pottery by Nampeyo. These pieces are thought to have been
made between 1895 and 1910.

Zuni polychrome pottery made around 1910. Note the sculptured frog figure on the jar at the top and the frog, tadpole, and water bug design elements of the terraced bowl below. This unusual piece also contains two plumed (feathered) serpent figures which surround the frog. These pieces were probably used as ceremonial vessels.

Tesuque ceremonial bowl, at left, was made around the turn
of the century; jar, at right, about 1880.

Typical Santo Domingo pottery of the early 1900's.

Large polychrome jar, circa 1910, showing a number of typical design elements used in Zuni pottery.

Zuni pottery made between 1890 and 1910, displaying excellent examples of the deer with heart line and other traditional Zuni design elements.

Zia polychrome jar, circa 1895.

Two examples of rare Santa Ana polychrome pottery of the mid-to-late 1800's.

Santa Clara black and Santa Clara red pottery made around 1910.

Large Zuni polychrome storage jar, made sometime between 1910 and 1940, represents an unusually fine example of Zuni geometric pottery designs.

Pottery water jars (canteens) such as these have been used for centuries by Indians of the Southwest. Top, hanging: Acoma, circa 1900. Left background: large Hopi, early 1900's. Right background: very large Hopi, early 1900's. Left foreground: prehistoric Anasazi Culture, A.D. 1000 to 1200. Right front: Cochiti, circa 1900.

The polychrome jar, at top, was made in Zia Pueblo during the early to mid-1800's. The bowl was made around 1900 in San Ildefonso Pueblo by Martina and Florentino Montoya.

Zia polychrome pottery of the early 1900's. An old Navajo saddle of the same period is shown in the background.

San Juan pottery of the early 1900's.

San Ildefonso pottery jar made around 1914 by Maximiliana Martinez (older sister of Maria Martinez) and decorated by her husband, Crescencio Martinez.

Polychrome pottery by Maria of San Ildefonso Pueblo. Plate at top left was made by Maria and her son, Popovi, in 1966 and is signed "Maria/Popovi". The remaining pieces were made by Maria and her husband, Julian. Small jar at right was made around 1920 and signed "Marie". Large jar in foreground was made around 1910 and signed at a later date, "Maria Poveka/Julian".

An unusual black and red jar by Maria and her husband, Julian, made about 1920 and signed "Marie". The black jar with matte design is signed "Marie/Julian" and was made about 1930.

Examples of gun metal black pottery made during the 1960's
by Maria Martinez of San Ildefonso Pueblo. They are signed
"Maria Poveka". Popovi Da, Maria's son, assisted her during
the firing of these pieces.

Pottery made during the 1960's by Maria Martinez and her son, Popovi Da. Vase at left is sienna and black with a matte design. Jar at right is polychrome. Bowl in foreground is sienna with a matte design.

Lucy M. Lewis, well known potter of Acoma Pueblo, uses a gourd rind to scrape a freshly-formed pottery jar. As soon as the scraping is completed the jar will be sun-dried and then sanded. Lucy has been making pottery for over 70 years.

The Totem Poles in Monument Valley along the Arizona-Utah border.

Black-on-white styling of "Feather Woman", Helen Naha. Many of Feather Woman's designs are copied from pottery shards from the ancient Hopi ruin of Awatovi, which is near her home.

Traditional Hopi designs are accented with turquoise and coral in contemporary pottery by Hopi artist Wallace Youvella.

The creative styling of Hopi potter "Fawn", Eunice Navasie.

Santo Domingo pottery of the 1970's by Santana Melchor.

Contemporary styling of Thomas Polacca Nampeyo, grandson of Nampeyo and son of Fannie Nampeyo.

Pottery by "Frog Woman", Joy Navasie. Joy's mother, Paqua, the original Frog Woman, started the family tradition of making beautiful white pottery which is now carried on by daughters and granddaughters.

The magnificent pottery styling of Fannie Nampeyo, daughter of Nampeyo.

Three styles of pottery by Hopi potter Garnet Pavatea. Left: Black on red jar. Top right: Polychrome bowl. Right foreground: Corrugated red jar.

Pottery miniatures by a number of skilled pueblo potters.

Carved red and black pottery by Margaret Tafoya of Santa Clara Pueblo.

Pottery forms from Acoma Pueblo. The sheep, at top left, and owl with corrugated styling, at center, are by Jessie Garcia; the chicken and the owl with two babies by Marie Z. Chino and the turtle by Rose Chino.

Black-on-white wedding vase and pitcher were made by
Lucy Lewis of Acoma Pueblo in 1960. The design elements
of this contemporary pottery, including the animal effigy
handle, closely resemble designs used in prehistoric black-
on-white pottery. The large polychrome jar in the background was made around the turn of the century.

Unusual three-chambered vessel in foreground was made by Juana Leno of Acoma Pueblo. Large jar in background is prehistoric Tularosa Black-on-white, made between A.D. 1100 and 1250. Note the resemblance in designs. Many Acoma potters utilize ancient pottery designs in their modern work.

Helen Cordero of Cochiti
Pueblo is best known for her
pottery storyteller figurines.
This storyteller contains 25
children.

Old traditional Cochiti pottery styling is reflected in these recent pieces by Laurencita Herrera.

Carved jar, at the top, was made by Virginia Ebelacker of Santa Clara Pueblo. The large jar at the bottom contains a classic bear claw design and was made by Virginia's mother, Margaret Tafoya.

A section of Acoma Pueblo forms the setting for this beautiful Acoma pottery. The long necked vase with deer design and jar with bird design were made by Rose Chino. The remaining pieces were made by Rose's mother, Marie Z. Chino.

Grace Medicine Flower of Santa Clara Pueblo creations.
The small vase at the left is only 1¾″ tall.

Santa Clara pottery. Bowl, at left, and vase, at right, were made by Margaret and Luther Gutierrez (brother and sister). Plate in the center was made by Lela and Van, their mother and father.

Pottery styling of Grace Medicine Flower. This double-exposed photograph shows two views of this finely executed seed jar.

Pottery jar with matte design made in 1968 by Santana and Adam Martinez of San Ilde-fonso Pueblo.

Graceful, long necked polished black vase made by Rose Gonzales of San Ildefonso Pueblo.

Pottery by Mohave potter Elmer Gates. Mohave pottery often resembles that of the ancient Hohokam. The rattlesnake which is carved in relief on the jar at the right is similar to the carved rattlesnake motif found on Hohokam stone vessels. The broken pottery shards are remnants of prehistoric Hohokam red-on-buff pottery.

San Juan pottery by Tomasita Montoya and Dominguita
Sesneias is contrasted by a Navajo concha belt.

Central Arizona desert homeland of the Maricopa Indians frames these four Maricopa vessels. The polychrome bowl at the left is by Alma Lawrence. The wedding vase is by Grace Monahan. The tall long-necked vase is by Barbara Johnson and the long-necked vase, at the right end, is by Ida Redbird.

Pinon pitch-covered Navajo pottery by Fae Tso rests on a
Ganado Red Navajo rug by Alice Begay.

Old and new Zia pottery containing classic Zia bird designs. Large storage jar at the right was a utility piece made around the turn of the century. Jar, at left, is a smaller version made in 1974, primarily to be sold to collectors.

Micaceous pottery is common to the pueblos of Taos and Picuris, and is occasionally made in Tesuque. The old jar on the left was made in Taos Pueblo. The bowl in the background, also from Taos, was made by Virginia Romero. The deep bowl at the right with animal effigies and human faces is from Tesuque Pueblo.

The shifting sands of the Navajo land in northern Arizona.

Fannie Nampeyo, the daughter of Nampeyo of First Mesa in the Hopi reservation. Fannie is painting one of her pottery jars using a strip of yucca as a brush. Paints are made by boiling certain local plants.

Contemporary pottery styling by Minnie of Santa Clara Pueblo.

Salado Red human effigy, 7″ in height, is wearing necklace adorned with shell and turquoise. Made between A.D. 1100 and 1400.

Kinishba Polychrome made by descendants of the early Mogollon people of Arizona and New Mexico shortly after A.D. 1300.

Prehistoric Hopi bowls, jars and ladles, include black-on-yellow, black-on-orange and polychromes, made between A.D. 1300 and 1625.

Large Tonto Polychrome storage jar, Salado Culture, A.D. 1375-1450.

Anasazi storage jar 13″ in diameter. Pottery type is Kayenta Black-on-white, A.D. 1250-1300.

Great Land of the Nomads, thus the ancient Indian farmers and potters of the fertile valleys of Mexico called the country to the north. And at the center of the great land is the region we now call the American Southwest.

Here, elemental forces of heat and cold, wind and water, shaped the earth, forming monumental cliffs and rock canyons, mountains and mesas, broad plateaus and vast expanses of desert sands. It is a land of sharp contrasts and vivid colors, of gold and yellows and reds made bright in the clear air. Here are the varied greens of fir and spruce, pinon pine and juniper, of verdant bits of valley, of mesquite, cactus and wild grasses. Here are the ant and the insect creatures, the horned toad, lizard and rattlesnake, the butterfly, bluebird, crow and eagle, the deer, rabbit, coyote and mountain lion. And over all there is the sky, with sun bringing the many changing lights, the white of dawn, the blue of day, the yellow of evening and, in leaving, the black of night.

It was known also as the land of little water, but there are springs and streams and rivers, among them those we now call the Colorado, San Juan and Rio Grande, Verde, Salt and Gila. In time, the ancient nomads began to put down roots, and, like the wanderers of the Biblical deserts, to beget the ancestors of the present-day Indians of the Southwest.

Some two thousands years ago, corn-based cultures had developed throughout the region. There were similarities, and also differences on which the archeologists have based their designations of three major groups: Hohokam (Pima Indian word for "those who are gone"), Mogollon (for the mountain regions), and Anasazi (Navajo for "ancient ones," although they are not ancestors of the Navajos).

The Hohokam, the presumed ancestors of the Pima and Papago, occupied the desert valleys of southern Arizona from about 300 B.C. to about 1400 A.D. and engineered great canal systems to irrigate their fields with water from the Gila and Salt rivers.

The Mogollon, who were assimilated into other groups before the arrival of the Spanish in the 1500's, cultivated the highland regions and valleys in southwestern New Mexico and southeastern Arizona.

The Anasazi, whose early periods are referred to as Basketmaker and whose cultural history extends into the Pueblos of today, planted their crops near springs and streams and built their villages along mesas, cliffs and canyons in the vast plateau country of southern Colorado and Utah and northern Arizona and New Mexico.

Pottery came with the cultivation of the fields, when a wandering peoples joined themselves to a section of the land. For nomadic groups moving from place to place on foot, there would be little reason to replace baskets, skins or gourds, and to burden themselves, with easily broken pottery.

The earliest pottery yet found in the Southwest has been in sites of the Hohokam and dates from around the third century B.C. The form and finish of the pieces indicate considerable skill in pottery-making, none of the crude efforts of a beginner, and it is assumed that knowledge of the craft was brought in from northern Mexico where it had been practiced for several centuries.

Pottery was a long time developing with the Anasazi; first examples date from around the fifth century A.D., several hundred years after that of the southern peoples. The first rough pieces and the method of firing in a reducing atmosphere suggest that the Anasazi had evolved their own methods of pottery making without the benefit of the technical skills of the Hohokam or Mogollon. However, Mogollon vessels have been found in early Anasazi sites, so that some of the northern peoples were acquainted with the pottery, if not the technology.

The movement of peoples did not stop with the establishment of agricultural communities and the making of pottery, but continued, with time and conditions leading to the building of new centers and the disappearance of old.

Some of the Mogollon shifted to the north into the valleys of the Tularosa and San Francisco and towards the White Mountains (and after 1100 referred to as Western Pueblo), where they met with branches of the Anasazi considered ancestors of the Zuni and Hopi. Others moved towards the west and their Hohokam neighbors. And a group traveled into the lower Mimbres Valley towards Mexico.

The Salado (named with the Spanish word for salt) began appearing in the Tonto Basin Region of east central Arizona around 1100 A.D., and along the Salt where they farmed alongside the Hohokam, and subsequently into the region of the Verde. Their culture reflected elements of the Mogollon as well as contacts with the Anasazi. Little is known of them after 1450 A.D.

In the great region of the Anasazi there were the peoples of Mesa Verde and of Chaco Canyon who moved towards the Rio

Grande, and some towards the mesas of northern Arizona; there were those in the area the Spanish called Cibola, who formed the western pueblos; there were the Kayenta, ancestors of the Hopi, who traveled along the Little Colorado River and established villages along the southern border of the Colorado plateau. And there were others, who for a brief period, worked the black lava-covered soil near the Sunset Crater in northern Arizona. And by about 1400, the Pueblo peoples had settled in the locations where they are today: the Hopi villages, the Zuni villages and the Rio Grande pueblos.

The Navajos (and the Apaches) were late-comers to the land—the last of the nomads. After their years of wandering, the Navajos called this "the promised land." They learned from the "Dwellers in the Earth," as they named the Indians of the Pueblos and, in time, shared in a heritage based upon the earth and sky, soil and water, and a seeking for harmony with all things in nature.

Let the white floating clouds water the earth. Let the Sun embrace the earth that she be fruitful. Let the lightning, thunder and rainbow people water the earth. Let the lion of the north, bear of the west, badger of the south, wolf of the east, eagle of the heavens call to the Cloud People that the earth may be watered. Medicine bowl, cloud bowl, and water jar give us your heart that the earth may be watered. I make the ancient road of meal that my song may pass straight over it. (Zia rain song)

Soon after they began making pottery, the Indians of the Southwest began to decorate it. The painted decorations show a remarkable similarity in the design elements and forms used throughout the region, and in the sequence of their appearance. There are variations in the decorations that can be ascribed to the local group, and also to the individual artist whose personal vision and skill interprets the designs, just as the artists of today create their own styles. Differences in color depend, in good part, on the clay and materials available to the potter.

At first, the designs are geometric motifs, such as lines, squares, frets, circles, spirals and scrolls; then life forms, such as animals, reptiles, birds, plants and humans; and combinations of these motifs.

Archeologists have given names to the various pottery types based upon the locations where they have been found and the colors used. Within the Hohokam culture there are: Estrella (1-200 A.D.) and Sweetwater (200-350 A.D.) red-on-gray pottery on which simple geometric designs appear, triangles, broad lines or hatchings; Snaketown (350-550 A.D.) red-on-buff, with snake, lizard, bird and human forms; Gila Butte (550-700 A.D.), Santa Cruz (700-900 A.D.) and Sacaton (900-1100 A.D.) red-on-buff, with combinations of life forms and geometric designs.

Sometime after 1100, the Salado were producing Gila and Tonto Polychrome with black and white geometric designs on red backgrounds. (Polychrome, in pottery, generally refers to pieces on which more than two colors appear, including the slip, painted decoration and the color of the body clay, if it is purposely left unslipped.)

The Mogollon made use of geometric designs throughout most of their culture, producing brown ware and red ware with red decorations. Around 700 A.D. some pieces were painted with red on a white background and beginning about 950 A.D., black-on-white. Mimbres black-on-white (circa 1050-1200) presented striking life forms, including fish, in amazing variety, birds, deer, rabbit and insects.

First design motifs of the Anasazi were derived from those used in baskets, and included various linear forms, squares, triangles, and step-figures. Later scrolls, spirals, and circular figures were added. Birds, including parrots, animals, insects, were in use beginning around 1300. Within the region of the Anasazi there were many cultural groups who produced a variety of painted wares, including: Mesa Verde black-on-white, Chaco black-on-white, and Cibola and Little Colorado Whiteware. There were the black-on-whites of Reserve and Walnut, Tusayan, and Kayenta. And beginning around the twelfth century there were the Polychromes of St. Johns, Wingate and Show Low. And the striking early Hopi pottery named Jeddito black-on-yellow and the polychromes of Bidahochi and Sikyatki. There were many others, and the very number and quality of styles attest to the creative genius of the Indian potters.

Although there is similarity in the designs used by the many peoples, their meaning—or lack of meaning—as symbols undoubtedly varied from group to group. Designs which orginally had symbolic meaning may have been, in later times, used only as decorative features. And what were originally elements of design may be given meaning as symbols, as has been done on occasion to add romance to a particular piece of Indian art.

The designs of the Indian potters have a validity of their own and are pleasurable as works of art. But, over the years, various meanings have been ascribed to some of the symbols.

There is a rhythmic pattern which flows through the life of the Indian and it can be seen in the dances and songs and ceremonies as well as in the pottery. It is a tribal pattern which flows out of water from the earth and sky and grows out of the earth, the sources of life and food—and the materials of pottery.

Many of the symbols relate to water: lines in wave-like patterns, semi-circles in rainbow and cloud forms, a double staircase for clouds, forked lines and zig zag lines for lightning, a line with shorter lines falling from it for rain. A wavy line can also refer to the water serpent or feathered water snake, the guardian of springs and streams. The plumed serpent is a powerful symbol and appears in many design forms. According to a Tewa legend, the serpent threw itself across the sky at one time and from this came the Milky Way. The combination of bird and serpent symbolize the power of sky and earth. Feathers are left at springs during ceremonies and feather patterns appear in many pottery designs. The feathered serpent is also found in the Quetzalcoatl of Aztec mythology; *quetzal*, a tropical bird; *coatl*, a reptile.

Squares can refer to the four seasons, the four winds, the four directions. Rows of small squares can mean villages and squares joined together with lines can suggest families which are related. Groups of small squares with dots in the centers indicate corn.

Lines forming steps are used for mountains and fret designs for mesas and canyons. The wind and whirlwinds, the dust devils of the Southwest, are shown by spirals and circles. Inverted pyramids are said to indicate whirlwinds as they descend the canyons. A stepped or terraced figure is a symbol for earth and an inverted terrace is the sky.

The swastika is a design which has been used throughout the world since prehistoric times. The word is from the Sanskrit meaning "good luck." It has appeared on Southwest Indian pottery from the Hohokam to the Hopi, for whom it is a symbol of the migrations from the four directions of the universe to the center, which is the land of the Hopi. Circles and spirals were formed as the people came closer to their home.

Frogs, tadpoles, fish and dragonflies are symbols of water, and stars and suns are signs of the sky.

Many of the animal forms are symbols of the clans, and may also represent the idea of food or good hunting, or the particular force or strength found in the animal. In paintings of the deer,

a life-line is drawn from the mouth to the heart and space is left around the line as the trail for the breath of life.

The hump-backed flute player appears on pottery of the Hohokam, and for the Hopi, he is said to have brought good harvest and happiness.

The kachina (katcina, kacina) are the forces of nature.

On some of the decorated pottery, the ends of a circle around a vessel do not quite close, leaving an opening as the exit trail for the life or being.

And it is said that each pot has a voice which can be heard when the pot is struck or when it is simmering on the fire. And if the pot cracks or breaks, that is the sound of the voice as it leaves, for the pot will never ring clearly as it did when it was whole.

Whether meaningful symbol or decorative pattern, there is beauty in the work, and inspiration in an enduring creative power. For out of the earth of the American Southwest, the Indian women of ancient days began forming their pottery, and with their craft shaped an art and tradition which continue to live in the creative hands of the Indians of today.

First Man and First Woman led The People into the new world. They came to a river and made some of the waters run on the land, planted the corn seeds they had brought with them and told their sons, the Changing Twins, to watch over the fields. One Twin saw some reeds growing near the river. He picked them and wove them into a water basket. The other Twin noticed some earth of a different color. He put some of the earth in the palm of his hand and it shaped into a bowl. Then, he formed a plate and a ladle. (from a Navajo myth)

The materials and methods in use today are essentially the same as those of the ancient potters. Clay is found along banks of streams, in valleys and washes and in deposits in what may have been ancient lakes and waterways. A variety of kinds and qualities of clay are found throughout the region; those in the southern and central areas tend to fire a reddish brown and those in the northern areas, gray and off-white. Some of the clays in the Hopi lands produce a warm tan and those around Acoma a dense white. Some of the sedimentary clays along the upper Rio Grande are red-firing and clays in some deposits in the Galisteo Basin are buff-firing.

The clay is dug from the earth in big lumps. It is then pounded into a powder and cleaned of bits of stone and gravel, twigs and fibers which cause imperfections or air pockets in the firing of the pots. Tossing the powdered clay into the air from blanket to blanket was once one of the methods used in cleaning. Sifting screens, and sometimes even flour sifters, are generally used today. And the old stone pounding and grinding tools have been for the most part replaced by steel hammers.

Tempering materials are usually added to the clay in order to ensure a more even drying and firing of the vessels. Sand, pulverized potsherds, volcanic materials or stone, including in some cases, ground up granites and basalt are used as temper. Powdered mica, which has long been used, gives a glistening quality to vessels which may have led some of the early Spanish to believe that they were made of gold. Coarser tempers are usually found in the utilitarian vessels and finer tempers in the decorated wares.

Cleaned clay is mixed with tempering material and water until the mixture has the texture and feel that the potter wants. The correct formula is in the hands and experience of the potter. The mixture is thoroughly kneaded until the mass is smooth and free of air bubbles. To make sure that it is uniformly moist the clay is usually set aside to cure for a few days in a dampened sack or cloth. Prepared clay is also stored in wet wrappings to keep it from drying out.

Taking a lump of clay in hand, as did one of the Twins, and gradually hollowing it out and shaping it by squeezing and pressing with thumbs and fingers is a method we now call pinch pottery. It is still a popular way of introducing youngsters and beginners in ceramics to work with clay. If the clay is worked on a flat surface with both hands, small flat dishes and shallow bowls can be formed. Holding a small ball of clay in the palm of one hand, turning and working it with the other can produce a small hemispheric bowl.

With larger amounts of clay, this method of manufacture can result in some interesting variations in form. Supporting a bowl on its side with one hand, while using the other to turn it and thin and build up the walls, the base becomes conical. As the walls build up and the bowl is tipped more against the supporting hand, the base becomes more pointed. Though it is conjectural as to whether the Navajo Indians used this method, there are examples of their storage jars with pointed bottoms for which they wove circular fiber rings to support them or dug holes in the ground to hold them.

The position of the shaping hand can also produce changes in form. When the hand is on the far side of the pot (away from the potter), with the fingers on the outside working against the thumb, the wall tends to curve inward, resulting in a mouth opening smaller than the central body of the vessel. With fingers working on the inside, the upper part of the vessel tends to flare outward and the pressure of the thumb on the outside will produce a flared rim.

Prior to the time Anasazi began making pottery, they made crude vessels of a sort during the early Basketmaker period, by mixing mud with vegetable fibers and molding it inside baskets, and sometimes just shaping it with their hands, to form thick-sided dishes which were dried by the air and sun. Some fire-hardened fragments of mud vessels have been found in burned ruins of Basketmaker dwellings, but no examples of true fired pottery. Later, baskets served as molds for the bottoms of pots and the bodies were built up by the coil method. Open fires were used for hardening. It is interesting to note that the term for potter used by the natives of southern Nigeria means "weaver of pots."

Clay Old Woman mixed clay with sand and softened it with water. She made it into a ball and wrapped it in a white shawl. She began to coil a pot with her clay. And all the people gathered in the village and watched her all day long. When she had made her pots about eighteen inches high, Clay Old Man, who had been singing and dancing beside her, kicked one and it broke in many pieces. Clay Old Woman took the broken pot and rolled it into a ball again. Clay Old Man gave a piece of it to everybody in the village. They each took it and made pottery as Clay Old Woman had made it. This was the time they learned to make pottery. In those days they only indented it with the marks of their fingers. (from a Cochiti legend)

The coil method—building up a vessel with coils of clay fitted one on top of the other—became the prevalent technique in forming pottery in prehistoric times and continues so today. The potter—traditionally a woman, though in recent years a few men have become skilled artisans—forms the base in one of several ways: by hand-forming the clay into a shallow bowl shape; by shaping a flat, circular biscuit, sometimes referred to as a tortilla; or by molding over the base of an existing bowl.

Next, a lump of the moist clay is rolled between the palms of the hands, gradually working it into a long, flexible rope or coil of the desired width. The coil is carefully pressed around the edge of the base and spiraled around and up, with additional coils being pinched and pressed on to build the vessel to the shape and height desired. Care is taken that the end-joins of the coils do not form a line up the side of the vessel, but are at different places around the circumference of the piece. The clay is kept moist and the fingers are frequently dipped in water to help in joining the coils and in rubbing the surfaces smooth.

The Hohokam used the paddle and anvil method to smooth and finish the surfaces of their pots. In this method a smooth, rounded stone or a piece of pottery is held against the inside wall of the vessel to keep it from collapsing while the outside is pounded smooth with a wooden paddle.

The potters of the plateau and Pueblo regions thinned the walls of their wares and smoothed away the coil marks by scraping both inside and outside with a piece of gourd or pottery sherd. This coil and scrape method continues as the one most used by the potters of today. Though, just as some of the early Navajos used corn cobs to smooth their pots, some of the present-day potters make use of metal and wood, even knives and tongue depressors, as scrapers.

After the shaping, scraping and smoothing, vessels are set aside to dry, sometimes out in the sun, sometimes in the shade for a brief period and then in the sun or a warm place. After the preliminary drying (and if no cracks have appeared), the vessels are further smoothed by rubbing with sandstone (some of today's potters make use of sandpaper or emery paper) and moistened polishing stones. The pieces can be fired at this stage, or, as is the case with most of the pottery today, decorated and then fired.

One form of decoration, as with the pottery of Clay Old Woman "indented with the marks of their fingers," appeared in early vessels of the Mogollon and the Anasazi groups and continued for several centuries. The coils were smoothed on the interior of the vessels, but became decorative elements on the exterior, in what is now called indented corrugated pottery.

The surfaces were manipulated in a variety of ways while the clay was still moist. Coils were pinched into wavy lines, indented in designed patterns of triangles and squares, incised with dots and lines. There were combinations of smooth surfaces and coils, of pinched corrugated coils and plain coils. The size of the coils was also an element of design. One bowl found at Gila Pueblo shows sixteen coils to an inch, with each coil distinct.

This mode of decoration also provided practical surfaces for utility vessels: they would be less apt to slip when handled and cooking pots would heat more quickly than smooth vessels because of the greater exposed area. This type of decorative treatment of cooking vessels continued until about 1300 A.D., when plain surface pots became prevalent.

Some potters today are producing their own distinctive versions of corrugated and incised designs on decorative pottery. *. . . there was some very beautiful glazed earthenware with many figures and different shapes. Here they also found many bowls full of a shining metal with which they glazed the earthenware. In all these provinces they have earthenware glazed with antimony and jars of extraordinary labor and workmanship, which were worth seeing.* (from the Coronado expedition journal, 1540)

Painted decoration appeared soon after or, perhaps, alongside the incised and corrugated pottery. Examples have been found in some ruins of painting done over corrugated surfaces.

On the painted pottery, until around 500 A.D., slip was not used; but in subsequent periods, slip was used to provide a foundation for the painting, to change the natural color of the clay, or to work as an element in the design.

Slips are made by mixing fine ground clays with water to a cream-like consistency. Yellows, browns, oranges and reds can come from earths containing mixtures of iron oxides; yellow ochre and red ochre are two of these. As limonite and hematite, they are often found with turquoise, and when they flow through it in network-like patterns, the stone is known as spider web turquoise. Bentonite, a clay formed by the decomposition of volcanic ash, can be used to make a cream or buff-colored slip.

The best white comes from a fine white clay called *kaolin*, which is used in making porcelain. The name was given by the French in the eighteenth century upon first receiving a quantity of the clay from the mountains in north China called Kaoling (high hill). Some of the finest kaolin deposits in the American Southwest are in the Acoma area. It is from here that the Zuni obtain the white used in painting their kachina figures. There are indications that the Mogollon imported this clay for use on their black-on-white pottery.

Slip is applied with a soft cloth, a rabbit tail, or, in some cases today, with a soft brush. While the slip is moist, the surface of the vessel is polished with small, smooth stones. These polishing stones are valued possessions of the potters, many of them are heirlooms passed from generation to generation. Stones, bearing signs of white and of red in small cracks, and similar to those which fit the hands of potters today, have been found during excavations of ancient ruins. Story has it that Maria of San Ildefonso used polishing stones which she and her husband Julian had discovered in an ancient cave. Some potters also use soft leather for final buffing.

To achieve the highly polished surfaces of the polished black and red ware, the burnishing can take several hours. For some pieces, slip is applied both to the interior and exterior. Sometimes the interior is also polished, and occasionally, only the rim or neck.

Slip is used, on occasion, only on one section of the vessel in order to provide a contrast between the color of the slip and the natural color of the clay. Two different colors—and sometimes more—are used as elements in the decoration of a vessel, particularly with some of the incised designs today. And some pottery today is accented with slips which produce blues and greens.

In general, the Hopi do not use slips on their traditional painted pottery because of the fine quality of their clay. Slips were used on the Polacca Polychrome.

On some pottery, the slip is only slightly buffed in preparing the surface for the painted designs.

The pigments for painting the vessels were, and are, made from a variety of mineral and plant materials. Limonite (yellow ochre) can be used for colors ranging from russet to yellow. Hematite (red ochre) is used as a red pigment. This was the red paint used by the Spanish ladies of Santa Fe as rouge during the seventeenth and eighteenth centuries. Governor of New Mexico de Vargas thought it might be cinnabar, which is a source of mercury used in the processing of silver. In 1692, he obtained a quantity of the material from the Hopi, who had long been trading with the Havasupai Indians near the Grand Canyon for their supplies of the red pigment. Analysis by the Spanish showed that it was hematite. Magnetite is a black iron ore which turns to red in an oxidizing fire.

Pyrolusite (manganese dioxide), which is found in the Zuni area, can be ground and used to produce a black. Black is also made from the leafy stems of Rocky Mountain bee plant (which the potters of San Ildefonso gather in early summer), or from tansy mustard. The plant materials are boiled until most of the water is evaporated and the remaining liquid is of a thick syrup-like consistency. The Hopi also produce a black using the tansy mustard liquid and adding powdered hematite. The Papago make a black by boiling mesquite bark which has darkened where sap has oozed out and adding clear mesquite gum as a binder.

Poster paints and acrylics are now used by some pueblos, such as Tesuque, Jemez and Isleta, where the strictly-for-tourist pieces are fired, sometimes in an ordinary stove oven, and then painted with a variety of designs in bright colors.

From around 1300 A.D. to 1700 A.D., a glaze paint was developed from ores containing lead. During the early years of the period, a Western Pueblo group in the Little Colorado River valley used a glaze paint in which copper was also an element and produced a red pottery with glossy black designs. Major production of glaze paint was in the Rio Grande pueblos around the Albuquerque region. Indications are that the glass-like paint was made from cerrusite, a carbonate of lead, which is found in mountain areas near the Galisteo Basin. The glaze was used generally to outline and accent designs. At the beginning of the period, the glaze was heavily pigmented and was only semi-glossy, becoming subsequently lighter and more transparent, until the late years of its use, it tended to run during firing and obscure the designs. Production of glaze-paint ware stopped, it is believed, because the Spanish had taken control of the mines from which the ore had been obtained. It is a forgotten skill in the pueblos of today.

Traditionally, the paint brush is made from a short piece of yucca stem, which has been chewed until only a few of the fibers remain. Today, many potters use store-bought brushes, from which they will oftimes remove some of the bristles.

It was Spider Woman who first taught the women how to use clay to make storage jars for food and water. In the beginning the jars were easily broken because the people did not have fire to harden them. Then, Butterfly came and showed them how to make fire with a bow-drill. And one time they were careless and their fire burned down a house. When the people searched the ashes, they found their clay pots had become hard. And so it happened that the people learned how to use fire to make their pots and jars hard and not so easily broken. (from a Hopi legend)

The Indian potters of the Southwest literally burn down a small structure each time they fire their pottery. They have never used a permanent kiln (though today, some students are becoming acquainted with kilns in school), but for each firing, the potters carefully construct a temporary and transitory structure around and over their pots, using available fuels and sherds and pieces of metal.

During the early periods of their pottery making, the Anasazi controlled the combustion of their fires by limiting the free flow of air and the supply of oxygen. This reducing atmosphere, as it is called, was unique with the Anasazi and resulted in vessels which were gray in color, light enough sometimes, to be called white. And if sufficient carbon were present the pots would smudge or become black.

The Mogollon and Hohokam, and the people of the Pueblos at a later period, fired their wares in an oxidizing atmosphere, wherein the fuels are permitted to burn freely and the air fans the flames. This was the method in use in Mexico and the Americas and is the method in general use today in the Southwest. Pots fired in an oxidizing atmosphere become red, brown, orange or white, depending upon the amount of iron in the clay.

Both the potters and pots undergo the test of fire. It is a fateful time when the work of many days is in the power of unknown forces. The potters' concern at firing is universal. The great Greek ceramicists of the time of Plato and Aristotle feared a demon who cracked pots while they were being fired, so they fixed a hideous Gorgon mask to the kiln to scare the demon away. Many of today's Pueblo potters can remember when their grandmothers would sprinkle corn meal or pollen over the stacked vessels and around the fire pile, singing a prayer that the pots would be good.

Firing is done outdoors, on a calm day so that the wind does not play tricks with the flames and smoke. On a clear, level place a fire is built to create a bed of coals to serve as a base for the pots and the final fire. Fuel can be bark, chips and pieces of wood from cedar or juniper, chunks of local coal, and dried manure, usually sheep, though cow and horse are also used. Over the leveled bed of coals, an even layer or two of fuel is spread and then flat pieces of broken pottery, stone or even pieces of tin or metal are placed to make a floor or grate on which the vessels to be fired are carefully placed upside down. There are often two and three layers of pots stacked up.

Large pieces of broken pottery and/or sheets of tin are placed around and over the pots to protect them from the flames and burning fuel. Fuel is piled up to cover and enclose the assembled structure so that fire completely envelops it. After the fire has burned out, nothing is touched until everything has gradually cooled. A sudden change in temperature, bringing a vessel hot from the flames into cooler outside air, may cause the piece to crack. Cooling usually takes several hours, sometimes overnight.

Removing the fired pots from the ashes is the moment of truth and a tense one. The good pots will give off a clear tone when tapped; a dull thud from a pot or jar usually indicates a crack or imperfect firing. Dark smudges, called fire clouds, sometimes appear on the sides of vessels where they have been touched by flames or smoke. On painted pottery, the fire clouds can ruin a design, but often, on plain pottery, the clouds can be a decorative element. On occasion, a wayward stream of smoke may flow over a pot long enough to turn it black.

Since the early 1900's, the pueblos of Santa Clara and San Ildefonso have intentionally been producing polished black ware. During the final stages of firing, the blaze is smothered by heaping on powdered manure, producing a dense, carbon-filled smoke which coats the red-hot pottery with black.

Although polished black and matte black ware are among the best known of present-day pueblo styles, black pottery and vessels with polished black or carbon-smudged interiors dating back a thousand years have been found. This surface treatment of the pieces may have been used, in part, to make the pottery less porous. If the earthenware is too porous, it will not hold liquid very long and is not suitable for water storage. However, some porosity permits slow evaporation through the walls of the vessel, and in warm climates help keep the water cool. The use of carbon on the interiors of vessels could also have been a way of protecting them and of keeping the water fresh.

Today, the Navajos coat the interiors of some of their few large water jars with creosote or pinyon pine pitch, just as they coat the inside and outside of their woven water carriers, or pitch baskets.

The women busy themselves only in the preparation of food, and in making and painting their pottery and baking pans in which they prepare their bread. These vessels are so excellent and delicate that the process of manufacture is worth watching, for they equal, and even surpass, the pottery of Portugal. The women also make earthen jars for the carrying and storing of water. These are very large, and are covered with lids of the same material. (from the diary of Herman Gallegos, describing the Tiwa south of present-day Albuquerque in September 1581)

Utility vessels for the preparation, serving and storage of food and for the transport and storage of water were produced by the ancient potters from the time they first began to work with clay. There were variations in shape from region to region and from period to period, but the bowl and jar have continued as basic vessels from the earliest times through today. The Spanish word *olla* is often used to refer to water jars, and sometimes to other storage jars, though in Spain and Latin America it usually designates a plain cooking pot.

Jars for bringing water from springs and streams would vary in size and shape depending in part on the method of transport. Some ancient ruins have contained large wide-mouthed jars with remnants of yucca leaf straps around them, straps which would be suitable both for carrying and hanging the jars. There were narrow-necked jars with handles on either side of the large round bodies for use in lifting and pouring, and for help in balancing when the jar is being carried on the head. The bottoms were often concave, which would help the jars fit the shape of the head.

Ancient woven fiber rings, like giant napkin rings, have been found which are similar to the pot rests woven of yucca leaves used by some of the pueblo women today as supports for round-bottomed jars when placed on their heads or on the floor.

Navajo legends tell of bottles or jars of white, blue, yellow and black, the four sacred colors, used to carry water from the four sacred mountains. These jars were flattened on one side and had looped handles on either side of the narrow neck. A rope could be passed through the loops to help in carrying the jars. Hopi legend tells of the magic water jar given to the clans by the guardian spirit, Masaw or Masauwu. They were to carry it with them in their migrations over the earth and when they found themselves in a land without water, they were to plant the jar in the ground and water would flow out of it. A plain, undecorated vessel which the Hopi have long made is a large, round canteen with the handles or lugs and small, elongated neck adjacent to the flat side.

Canteens and water jars in a variety of sizes are produced today, though many are suitable only for decorative display. The hard-fired white ware of Acoma and Zia pueblos can hold water for long periods without being damaged. However, much contemporary pottery, including the polished red and black ware of San Ildefonso and Santa Clara, can be harmed by water. Coating the interiors with silicone sealer or varnish can offer some protection, but moisture can mar the exterior surfaces.

Ladles, dippers and mugs were early products of the pottery makers, but are not much in evidence today outside of museums. One of the Pueblo ruins on Weatherill Mesa in Mesa Verde National Park is named Mug House because of the quantity of mugs found there and on the mesa. It is thought that these decorated, heavy handled mugs were used for drinking soups or corn gruel.

Food bowls of various kinds, cooking pots and storage jars to protect corn and meal from rodents and moisture were in general use until recent historical times. Today many of the utility vessels have been replaced by factory-made products. The Hopi continue to make and use some cooking, serving and storage ware, which is well-fired, but rough-finished and undecorated. Of the cooking jars being made today, the best known are probably the bean pots of Picuris. These brown, mica-flecked pots, often smudged by fire clouds, are used by both Anglos and Indians for simmering beans and chili.

Pitchers in various shapes and sizes, some with effigy handles, double-necked vessels, and effigy vessels in bird, animal and human forms have been produced since the time of the ancients. These vessels, as well as many of the decorated bowls and jars, could have served for ceremonial use.

Today, double-necked vessels, some referred to as wedding jars, are made by many of the Southwestern potters. The marketplace now offers a variety of effigy-adorned and shaped vessels as well as pottery figurines such as the animal forms of Santa Clara and Cochiti, the owls which have been made at Zuni for almost a century, and the pottery people of Cochiti and Papago.

For almost three hundred years the Pueblo potters supplied the Spanish and Mexican colonists with most of their household pottery. The Spanish seemed to have had little effect on the techniques and styles of the Pueblo potters, other than in the addition of pitchers with pouring spouts and in the shape and size of some plates. For their own use, the Indians continued with their traditional vessels.

The conquest and colonization did result in the destruction of several pueblos and the Pueblo Revolt of 1680 with the subsequent reprisals led to the dispersion of some of the Indian peoples and the disruption of some pottery centers, such as those in the Galisteo Basin where glaze-painted ware had been produced.

The quantity of pottery manufactured for the Spanish must have been huge and the trade over the three centuries of ever-increasing importance to the economy of the pueblos. It has been estimated that just prior to American control of the territory, the Pueblo potters were producing enough wares to meet the pottery needs of some forty thousand people, in addition to those of their own people.

With the coming of the railroad in mid-nineteenth century, the household pottery supplied by the Indians was replaced more and more by the kiln-fired, glazed ironstone, stoneware and crockery from eastern factories.

The railroad also brought tourists who liked "things" Indian to take home with them, and dealers who catered to the tourists and made a market in souvenirs. The Indians who had adapted to many invasions over the centuries began to supply this new market with a variety of wares, many of them specifically requested by the curio dealers.

The country is flooded with cheap, and scientifically speaking, worthless earthenware made by Pueblo Indians to supply the tourist trade . . . Only those persons who happen to be familiar with the refined and artistic ware of the ancient Pueblos can appreciate the debasement brought about by contact with the whites. (W. H. Holmes, American Anthropologist, 1889)

During this same period and the years to follow, there were Indian potters who continued in the traditional way to build vessels of good quality, enlightened traders who provided a market for good works, and archeologists who were unearthing some of the "artistic wares of the ancient Pueblos."

Two of the potters, Nampeyo of Hano and Maria of San Ildefonso, are generally credited with having inspired the renaissance of Pueblo pottery making.

Nampeyo (sometimes spelled Nampeo, and on some of her pots Nam pa ye) was born about 1860 in the First Mesa village of Hano, which had been founded in 1696 by Tewa-speaking Indians from the Rio Grande area. She learned to make painted pottery from her paternal Hopi grandmother at Walpi, which at that time was the primary Hopi village producing other than undecorated utility ware. This painted pottery, in a style designated Polacca Polychrome and made from around 1800 to 1900, was the only slipped pottery made by the Hopi. It is sometimes referred to as "crackle-ware", because the heavy slip buckles and cracks when fired. As Nampeyo developed her skill as potter and painter, she often decorated her grandmother's work in addition to her own.

In 1881 she married Lesou (sometimes spelled Lesoo), a Hopi from Walpi. He joined with her in collecting and copying designs from ancient potsherds and there is some evidence that some of the designs were used on crackle-ware in the early 1890's.

Lesou was one of the Hopi men who worked for Dr. Jesse Walter Fewkes during the excavation of the ruins of Sikyatki in 1895. It was here that early Hopi people created Sikyatki polychrome pottery from the late fourteenth century to the early seventeenth. The clay of the pottery was fine-grained and fired to a buff or yellowish-brown color, which is customarily designated as yellow. Black and red were used in painting the bold designs and stylized birds, feathers and butterflies on the curved surfaces of the mortuary bowls, jars and sherds found in the Sikyatki ruins.

The quality of the pottery and the striking character of the designs captured the interest of Nampeyo and Lesou. They made many drawings of the old designs as the pieces were unearthed. But Nampeyo went beyond this. She searched out the source of the clay and after many experiments found what she considered the right mixture. She also worked to obtain the materials for the same colors of paint.

She soon began producing pieces which were close copies of the Sikyatki Polychrome, and as she grew in mastery of the style, she developed a freedom in her own designing, a quality of creative expression, which marked the beginning of a new era in Hopi pottery making. The new version of Sikyatki is sometimes referred to as Hano Polychrome.

Nampeyo inspired the Hopi women of First Mesa and encouraged them in their own work. In 1898, and again in 1910, Nampeyo and her husband, Lesou, were taken by the Santa Fe Railroad Company to demonstrate pottery making at the Chicago Railroad Exposition. Her blindness, which began about 1920, became total between 1924 and 1925. She continued to form and polish pottery and Lesou began to paint the designs in the Sikyatki style with a skill which matched that of his wife. He was assisted by their daughters who were becoming adept in the craft, and who, upon his death in 1932, cared for their mother and helped her with her pottery. Nampeyo died July 20, 1942, but her creative force continues in the inspired work of her daughters, and their daughters, and the present-day Hopi potters.

Maria Montoya Martinez (or Marie Martinez), whose Indian name is Poh've'ka, was born about 1881 in the Tewa-speaking village of San Ildefonso, which the Indians called *p'owo'ge*, place where the waters meet (sometimes translated, in reference to the Rio Grande, where the waters cut through). She learned to make pottery from her aunt who lived in the pueblo; at first, plain smooth surfaced bowls and then, painted polychrome wares with a tan or cream slip and designs in black and red.

In 1904, she married Julian Martinez of San Ildefonso Pueblo and during that same year she travelled with him to the St. Louis Exposition where they were members of the Indian craft village and she demonstrated her skill in pottery-making.

During the summers from 1907 until 1910, Julian was a digger at the excavations being conducted by Dr. E. L. Hewett in the ancient ruins on the Pajarito Plateau. Both Maria and Julian were intrigued by the quality of the pottery and the designs which were discovered. When the Museum of New Mexico was organized in 1909, Dr. Hewett asked Julian to make reproductions of murals from a nearby ruin and copies of prehistoric pottery designs. It was during this period that Maria was employed to demonstrate pottery-making at the museum and that Julian began to paint some of her pottery.

Around 1913 they developed their own black ware (other Rio Grande pueblos had been producing black ware), following many experiments in firing. Maria's reputation for quality grew, as did the sales of her pottery, polychrome as well as polished red and black. At the 1915 Panama-California Exposition in San Diego, Maria and Julian worked at their pottery in the exhibition of Indian Pueblo crafts. They maintained their standards of excellence and were successful in producing some new pieces larger than they had attempted before. They were also successful in selling them, though they saw that the tourists seemed equally happy with poorly-made rain gods, candle sticks and gaudy curios.

The discovery of black-on-black or matte-and-polished black ware occured around 1919, when Julian painted a design on one of the slipped and polished pots Maria had ready for firing. When the pot was taken out of the ashes, the design was a flat black or matte against the shiny black of the polished surface. Further experiments gave them the knowledge and skill to pro- duce a matte background for polished designs. At first, Maria and Julian kept the secret to themselves, but then, in the early 1920's taught other potters in the pueblo how to produce the polished-matte black wares.

The work and the success of Maria, and of Julian, set an example for her sisters and other Indian potters, and helped build appreciation and respect for the Pueblo potterymakers and demand for their wares.

During the summer of 1934 at the Century of Progress Exposition in Chicago, Maria and Julian presented their pottery, and again in 1939 at the Golden Gate Exposition, San Francisco.

At the time of Julian's death in 1943, Maria's skill was already legendary. And the legend and her art have continued to grow with the years. In the early 1960's, she and her son Popovi Da perfected a new gunmetal finish which glistens with the quality of burnished silver. It is only recently that she has discontinued her pottery-making. However, the creative tradition she reestablished with her husband has continued through the work of her sons and her grandchildren, and the potters of the pueblos.

Antaeus was a giant of great strength, who had been conceived by Mother Earth. He lived in a cave beneath a towering cliff in the region of the mountain lions. And he slept on the bare ground, because only as he maintained contact with the earth did he stay strong. (from a Greek myth)

Maria and Nampeyo created a living legacy for the Indians of the American Southwest and began a cultural revolution. They learned from the art of the ancients and built on the two thousand year tradition of the Indian potters: of holding what was good, of reviving old styles, experimenting and making radical change.

Today, there are the styles and types of pottery for which each pottery-making pueblo is known—the orange-brown pottery of Picuris and Taos with the flakes of mica shining on the surface, the polished black and red wares, and the matte black, carved and incised designs, of Santa Clara, San Ildefonso and San Juan, the white ware of Acoma and Zia with decorative, conventionalized designs, the owls of Zuni and the polychromes of Hopi—but there are also the works of new potters in the pueblos and of Indians in other villages, artists who are creating new forms and new styles out of the earth of the Southwest. And keeping a tradition strong.

Acknowledgements and Appreciations

Ashton Gallery · Scottsdale, Arizona
Milt Coggins
Fenn Galleries Ltd. · Santa Fe, New Mexico
Gallup Indian Trading Company · Gallup, New Mexico
Gila River Arts & Crafts Center · Sacaton, Arizona
Harvey Collection/Heard Museum · Phoenix, Arizona
Heard Museum Collection · Phoenix, Arizona
Hunter's Trading Post · Phoenix, Arizona
William E. Hinkley
Hubbell Trading Post · Ganado, Arizona
Lee's Indian Crafts · Phoenix, Arizona
McGee Traders, Inc:
   Pinon Mercantile Trading Company · Pinon, Arizona
   Keams Canyon Arts & Crafts · Keams Canyon, Arizona
Lynn Pearlstein
Popovi Da Studio of Indian Arts · San Ildefonso Pueblo,
   New Mexico
Jack D. Rich
Salmon Ruins · San Juan County, New Mexico
Tanners Indian Arts · Scottsdale, Arizona/Gallup, New Mexico

Special Appreciation

Dr. Patrick T. Houlihan, Director of the Heard Museum,
   Phoenix, Arizona.
Jon Thomas Erickson, Curator of Collections · Heard Museum,
   Phoenix, Arizona
Ann Marshall, Assistant Curator of Anthropology · Heard
   Museum, Phoenix, Arizona
Cynthia Davies, Curator of the Harvey Collection · Heard
   Museum, Phoenix, Arizona
Robert Ashton
Gary Carlson
Jerold Collings
Laurens C. Hammack · Arizona State Museum
Richard M. Howard
Dennis Lyon
Wm. Bruce McGee
Richard L. Spivey
Dr. Cynthia Irwin-Williams · Eastern New Mexico University

*There is a spirit, it is said, in every beautiful jar. In a book
like* Pottery Treasures *there are many spirits: the spirits of those
who helped—with counsel, examples and encouragement—
and are now a part of its beauty. I am grateful.*

                           Jerry Jacka